Dedicated to the strangers

Thank you for your strangeness

Chemical

Messengers

Exary Valles

chemical messengers

chemical messengers

chemical messengers

chemical messengers

UNTITLED

I'm looking through my old

sketchbook

I found this funky dog thing

In a big jacket

Smoking a cigarette

With his drink on the floor

I can tell he has a hard time with

others

That's why he's alone

I'm going to tell you about my art

But I'm really telling you about

myself

chemical messengers

ROADKILL

A dog got hit by a car

There it lies

Slowly becoming two dimensional

The flow of traffic remains consistent

That roadkill had a name

chemical messengers

WILDER THINGS

We used to be animals

And when predator hunts prey, pure

romance

"Could you love someone when you know

they'll only ever hurt you?"

The coyote asks the rabbit by its teeth

around its throat

The rabbits blood coating the coyote's

mouth

the answer it feared and longed for: "Yes."

chemical messengers

BEAUTIFUL CANVAS

We were given such a beautiful canvas

Big open spaces, mountains, valleys, hills

Green grass, blue skies, white clouds

And we wrote our name on it in big letters

That's what we're here for

And one day, we'll be gone, and whatever

comes next will dig up our remains and say,

"Look, here they were. What did they do

with this?"

And I'll say,

Quiet enough that they can't hear,

We wrote our names in big letters.

Exactly like we were supposed to

chemical messengers

FUNCTIONAL ART

In a billion years

When we're all gone

The aliens will dig up the cern supercollider

Its ruins buried under tons of rock and ice

And they'll marvel at the artistry

Maybe they'll theorize

On the metaphor

"This large eye perhaps signifies the species'

curiosity. Perhaps, in such a lonely universe,

they meant to show that, despite their

isolation, they always found meaning."

chemical messengers

UNSENT LOVE LETTERS

This love only ever sends us to hell

There was another option

But listen:

Keep telling me you love me

And I'll make it hurt the whole way down

chemical messengers

THE FINAL PART OF A

SENTENCE IS A PERIOD

A period is the last part of a joke

A rant

A speech

A story doesn't end in words

Pieces of a syntax define it

A period comes after a sentence

It pursues it hungrily

Before humans and written words dinosaurs

walked the earth. (period)

An asteroid struck the earth. (period)

The debris blotted out the sky. (period)

 A blue marble turned black. (period)

A black dot. (period)

A period.

chemical messengers

A GHOST OF A GHOST

These new candles look like ghosts

And I think it's funny

A ghost- I say- is the remains of what once was

These brand-new candles resemble the remains

of what once was

And when they're lit,

They lose shape

I ask- what did you do with what was left?

"I threw it away."

A ghost, a shell of what once was

The entropy- it doesn't even look like a ghost

anymore

Now it really is a ghost

So it got thrown away

chemical messengers

UNTITLED

I'm returning your things

I want to leave a note with them

I won't

Remember those little love notes I'd hide in

your room?

I'll love you forever

You're my world

What a joke

I'm returning your things

And I know I can't tell you how you made

me feel

But if I left that note

I think it'd go something like

There's a reason everyone you've ever loved

has left

chemical messengers

Your abandonment issues were always a

self-fulfilling prophecy

Knowing I deserved better never made me

psychotic

We wanted to make each other better

All you ever did was make me worse

I loved you more than anything

You disgust me

And I hope I never have to see or hear from

you ever again

chemical messengers

HE'S NOT FROM AROUND HERE

"Oklahoma, huh? Welcome to civilization."

He laughs. He always laughs.

I don't know him well enough to like him

But I know that I like him

I like the way his hair curls

I like his laugh

I like his eyes

Because they're dead like mine

When I see myself reflected in them, I can't

help but look away

chemical messengers

GROWTH

What does growth look like?

Is it taking my meds every day?

Is it my fitted sheets?

My pillowcases?

Remember when I said I'm never getting

better?

The smoke from our cigarettes obscuring the

streetlights

Remember the blood on my wrists?

Red like our lips, like our tongues and the

words spilling out of my mouth

Where does it go after I wash it away? Even

when it's gone, it's not gone

chemical messengers

WILDER THINGS: THE RABBIT

LIKEWISE PREDATING

She watches the coyote watching her

A moments silence

Two pairs of eyes narrowing in concert

There's freedom in being hunted-

In literally running for your life-

Knowing that

Even if you get away

Even if you manage to evade that

Violent

Hungry

Thing

A mere pace behind you

This is the only part of your life That

chemical messengers

Ever

Fucking

Mattered

And for a moment-

Just a moment- you feel disappointment as

you shake your pursuer

chemical messengers

KURT TEACHES ME ABOUT MACHINES

Sydney's book, firsthand first now

secondhand tells me a story about a man

losing his mind

The words tell tales of human machines- the

arrangement of the words (carefully placed

thus so) tells me of psychedelic travels

which, before not too long ago would have

been unrecognizable

to me

Kurt has Kilgore Trout have God tell anyone

that they're the only sentient being in the

universe

Kurt has Dwayne Hoover take it personally

chemical messengers

Kurt has Dwayne bite Kilgore's finger clean

off

Through time and space, I feel Kurt's

idiosyncrasies match my own

I line them up artificially.

So it goes

chemical messengers

SOMEONE THAT LEFT

Escape artist meets escapist artist

Out of towner

I didn't know you long enough to fall as

hard as I did

Leave then

Muskogee, then Yakima, then

What

Elsewhere

Like lightning, I'll watch you follow the

path of least resistance

Somehow that means a quick and easy

egress

Fine then

chemical messengers

Not like I didn't live twenty years before

you

Still

A shared cigarette during the first cold snap

You and I, inches apart in a parked car in a

parks parking lot well past sunset

Next to one another at McDonalds

Two empty seats across from us

You liked that I write

I wrote this about you

You asked me what being in love meant to

me

"Someone who makes me feel something

I've never felt before"

I'd never felt lonely on behalf of another

person

chemical messengers

I'm grieving in your absence like you'll ever

be somewhere that feels like home again

I'm mad that you ran away so I don't feel

sad that you left

Leave then

I still wish I could've asked you to stay

chemical messengers

THERE'S A ███ GIRL

███████████████████

███████████ I was twelve █ I

would ██████ think about her

Sometimes █████████

████████ her ██████████

█████████████

███ clothes ██████████

████████ let her down ███████████

██████████ take us somewhere

█████ now, there's a ███ girl

██████████████

And ███ her ████

███████████████████

And █████████ I █████████

chemical messengers

▮▮▮ I dress ▮ up

▮ sometimes ▮▮ in front of the

mirror

▮ we look ▮▮▮

▮▮

And we ▮▮▮▮ felt safe

And ▮▮

Those ▮▮ eyes

Will leave ▮▮

▮▮▮ my mirror

But

▮▮

There's a ▮ girl ▮▮▮

▮▮

I ▮▮ think ▮ about her

chemical messengers

LOST TIME (PARENTHESES)

This is a love story told in parentheses

(this love story is: an interlude, an aside, a

digression)

I'm driving from Yakima to Tacoma

(all I can think about is how much I love

you)

I do the math

(pinpointing exactly when I get to you)

My car clock says 10:40

My map says

In eleven miles turn right

At sixty-five miles an hour

(barely speeding)

chemical messengers

I need to turn right when my car clock reads

ten fifty one

When my car clock reads 10:51 The time

will be 4:57

(this planet is five hours and fifty five

minutes ahead)

Two weeks ago, that meant four more hours

of sunlight

(today that means I get where I'm going at

dusk)

In less than twenty four hours, I convinced

myself you would choose me

(things are different now that I'm back)

Tell me how you feel

"This is the most fun I've had in a long

time"

chemical messengers

Late night phone calls

(make me your secret)

Tell me you want me

(why is it that the only things I ever have to

offer are my words and my body?)

I wanted to be your everything

(I'll settle for anyone's anything)

I picked you up from work

(I timed my departure so I could get there as

you get off)

Let's stay out all night

(I don't want to lose a second with you)

Somehow, I feel like I've convinced you

that you love me

(I've convinced myself that you're

convinced that you love me)

chemical messengers

You told me you don't think I'm

complicated

(I think it's time for me to go)

I'm driving from Tacoma to Yakima

(and all I can think about is how much I hate

myself)

chemical messengers

THIS USED TO BE SOMETHING ELSE

The house I grew up in is a different house

now

House to ashes to house again

The house we lived in after burnt down in

the fifties

Seventy years ago, the house I lived in used

to be a different house

This is your land

It used to be something else

Then we changed it

Now we're leaving

So, it's your turn

I'm thinking about that old country house

Its lawn disappearing beneath black walnuts

chemical messengers

And orange leaves

It used to be something else

In the back are two burnt out sheds

Beside them, a pile of lumber, overgrown

with sagebrush and goat head vines

Somebody tried to build something here

They're gone now

And slowly the evidence is disappearing

chemical messengers

DEVON THINKS SHE'D BE A GOOD CANDIDATE FOR A LOBOTOMY

I tell Devon I'm glad we exist

simultaneously

She asks me if I'm going to art school

Regret wraps itself around my

"No."

Devon shows me her art

She turns her art teacher into Christ at the

last supper

She asks if we're all fucked

I didn't know the context, but the answer

was obvious:

"Yes."

chemical messengers

She teaches me about my eyes

In the stories we tell about ourselves, we're

the antagonists

We play supervillain so we can pretend we

aren't hurt

Violent fantasies bely vicious vociferosity

I tell Devon we're like convergent evolution

Different formulas but the conclusion

remains the same

Devon tells me she disliked me because I

was interesting

Devon compliments me

Devon doesn't intend to

chemical messengers

THE ZOMBIES DESERVE

HAPPINESS TOO

I watch them walk amongst themselves

 I try to walk among them

They notice me

They don't notice themselves

I notice them

There's an experience I'm supposed to have,

so I'm having it

There's an experience they're supposed to

have, too

And I'm glad they're having it

chemical messengers

LSD PSA

This is your brain

This is your brain on-

Wow

Sorry

This is your brain on-

Wow, this is my brain!

Three pounds of fat and water means the

entire world

And it's beautiful

And it's complicated

But there's something there

And what is the world

I'm not apart from it

I'm a part of it

I can see things better now

chemical messengers

Like a newborn baby

And do you know how important you are?

And did you know that you and I and

everyone who's ever existed

have only ever existed to experience

ourselves?

And did you know that we're the universe

playing shadow puppets

with itself to keep from going insane? And

did you know I love you?

And do you know that by virtue of your

existence, the world is a better place?

And I'm so happy to experience it with you

chemical messengers

WHAT IS A ROCKEM SOCKEM ROBOT TO A GOD?

He and I were made identically,

Like Adam and Lilith

I don't understand what sinful life I must have

led prior to my conception to deserve this

Is this the only life I get?

The things violence makes us long for I miss

being forgotten on a shelf

WHAT IS A GOD TO A ROCKEM SOCKEM ROBOT?

It seems all I'll ever know is the feeling of his

fist against my face

There's no meaning

This couldn't have been someone's idea

Who could be so cruel?

When you're born with fists instead of hands,

it's impossible to pray

chemical messengers

LESSON

There's something I was supposed to learn from

you

Otherwise, we wouldn't have met

I learned something from you

By your side, in the hospital, I learned

something

In the parking garage, before, I learned

something

I learned something from you

Otherwise, you wouldn't have left

You taught me something

You couldn't help it

That means something

chemical messengers

I REMEMBER THAT FIRST HOUSE

I remember the rose bushes

I remember the blackberries growing wild across

the street

Me stumbling home at some early hour,

Bleeding from the blackberry thorns,

And happy as a clam

There's not a lot I miss about my childhood, But

I think about those blackberry bushes

I know they'll never taste as sweet as I

remember them

That's okay

They'll never taste that sweet again, and that's

okay

chemical messengers

A MANTRA

I am aware of the impact I have on others

Forgive me my words

The tree forgives the axe

And loves it in turn

Forgive me my actions

The horse forgives the bit and bridle

The dog forgives the collar

Forgive me my moods

The house forgives the lightning

As it burns, the house forgives the lightning

Life is easy

Forgive me my tired eyes

I don't mean to stare

I stare

I don't mean to

Alone

chemical messengers

Life is easy

In a room full of people, life is easy

Forgive me my words

Life is easy

In a crowded bed

Life is easy

Alone at night

Life is easy

Forgive me my heart

Its aching in my chest

Its hardening with time

But life is easy

Forgive me my thoughts

I defy them daily

The prisoner forgives the gallows as the ground

drops from beneath him

Forgive me

chemical messengers

IN THE STORY WE WROTE

ABOUT US

I was a Phuca

You were a Selkie

A Phuca is a dark, slippery thing

An anglerfish in the swamp

A Selkie is a seal person

Their seal coat disguises their difference

In the story we wrote about us we were still

outcast

Shrouded in disguise

The difference thematically between our

deuteragonists is more than subtext

The Selkie- the victim

The Phuca- the victimizer

chemical messengers

YOU'RE LOOKING AT ME LIKE YOU KNOW SOMETHING I DON'T

And I start to wonder if maybe you know

something I don't

At some point during this stream of

consciousness, I start to wish you'd cut me off

There's a slight tilt of the head followed by

some approximation of:

"No, that's actually not normal."

I start to wonder if maybe I'm losing my mind

"Do you ever feel like you're losing your

mind?"

And then:

"Not as often as you do."

chemical messengers

WILDER THINGS: MISSED CONNECTIONS

I was a coyote picking apart the wolf that had

been terrorizing the stags in our neck of the

woods

You were the stag that had had enough

It was glorious

I was awestruck as I watched you rear up and

slam those big powerful antlers on the fierce

predator

Just as quickly as it had started

The wolf creeping close,

You spotting her,

You crushing her,

Me eating her

I wish I could bring you dinner

chemical messengers

But you are an herbivore

I am a scavenger

The quick violence of my evolutionary

grandmother's execution

Was poetry in motion

I'd love to see it again.

She tastes like the violence she lived by

I wonder how you taste

It might have felt twisted eating the she-wolf;

she and I certainly knew each other though we

weren't close.

Ultimately, we were different kinds of

carnivores

Canis Lupus, Gray Wolf. A fierce predator. A

strong and violent carnivore, last modern

relative to the precursor to all canines.

chemical messengers

Canis Latrans, Coyote. Scavenger, trickster,

intelligent eater and maker of dead things.

Cervus Canadensis, Elk. Herbivore, large, prey.

Me, Latrans, my fallen relative; Lupus, her

killer, Canadensis.

I watched

I salivated

When I fed, her blood was warm

Her meat was warm

Her eyes not yet glazed as our dead get.

I watched as the crows circled

I'd gotten there first

Stag

I suspect I'll get to see more of you, yet

When I tell the she-wolf's pups of their mother's

death

Wolves are pragmatic

chemical messengers

Nature can't help itself

They won't want you dead because you killed

their mother

They'll want you dead because hurting a

member of the pack hurts the whole pack

I'd love to see more of your poetry

chemical messengers

IF YOU TAKE YOUR MEDICINE EVERY DAY, YOU'LL GET BETTER

Don't you want to get better?

I don't know what I'd do with myself

They gave my brother medicine for his handwriting

I wouldn't say it's helped

They make a pill that makes you on time for work

I have meds to combat the effects of my meds

Sometimes I wonder if medication is the right path

for me

My brain is designed with a certain function in mind

If I can find that function, maybe I won't need the

meds.

chemical messengers

I THINK THE LAST TIME I DID

ACID IS THE LAST TIME I DO

ACID

I think it did something irreparable in my brain

But it's okay

Because

It's still my brain

chemical messengers

IF LIFE WAS EASY AS ALL THAT

I wouldn't have written that poem

I guess that's why it's a mantra

It's aspirational

One time I barked for a pack of cigarettes

It didn't occur to me at the time that that was a

new low

I guess

In the moment, it doesn't

chemical messengers

BLACKOUT POETRY

She,

The hawk,

Bore the young rooster repeatedly, The body

fearsome.

The housewife's providence; Agitation,

Fidgeting.

"Listen, remember, tell." The countenance fixed.

A waif, a tempest. That night possessed faces hidden.

An awful thing smiling, betrayed, quivering. Only the

future knew,

The pink ribbon, a smile

Doomed.

He shuddered.

He shuddered.

God had willed a man eaten. On quiet footsteps, a

star shone.

chemical messengers

HOW CAN I BE CRAZY? I KNOW ALL THE RULES

The sick learn they are sick from the healthy

The day I was born, they gave me a number

The disordered man seeks order

The second we met, I started putting you in

boxes

I know what you are

I see the angels that move around us and the

demons that live inside our hearts

Why are you upping my antipsychotic?

chemical messengers

COMPLICATIONS

Complicated people complicate people

It's like an STD or a viral infection

I spent a minute putting bodies between us

It felt good and it felt really bad

But it was easy when it was

I think about how little I was worth to myself for

so long

I'm better now

I'm so much better now

chemical messengers

I ASKED YOU IF YOU EVER

WANTED TO GET MARRIED

It was a scary question, even if it wasn't exactly

a proposal

I want to be the only people in the world with

you

Is that crazy?

My whole life I've tried to surround myself with

people

But all I want is to be alone with you

I want to have been there for everything you've

ever experienced; I want to become a part of you

I want to make our missing pieces match

I want our siphonophores to love each other like

we do

chemical messengers

THERE'S A PIECE TO THE SHIP-

IT'S PIECE FULL

Last night I didn't sleep a bit

I feel as though my body is a sinking ship

Like patching holes in hulls

Something breaks, add chemicals

Adderall in the morning, at night, alcohol

In between, caffeine and nicotine

Top it off with something green

chemical messengers

CHEMICAL MESSENGER

I'll describe myself for you in two words

"Dopamine seeking"

Can I blame this on my parents?

My dad apologized to me for inheriting his crazy

I don't mind

To me, manic just means, "In love with life"

And there's no good reason I can't say, "No"

And there's no good reason I can't stop

Can I blame this on my parents?

I don't tell Devon this, but

People want to be like people like us

They cosplay our crazy

But get scared by its genuine face

Can I blame this on my parents?

Whether I'm up for thirty-six hours straight

writing

chemical messengers

Or whether I'm in the backseat of a stranger's car

There's something beautiful about madness

Something lovely about being incurably me

Can I blame this on my parents?

chemical messengers

WILDER THINGS: I KNOW WHAT YOU DO

I watch you watch her

She'd be pretty on the side of the road, I suppose

A hare to a coyote

A target to a gun

So, why?

You and I are the same type of thing

Eaters of the dead

We'd be magnificent

You, on land

Me, in the air

The things we'd find

So, why?

A coyote to a hare

A killer to a victim

So, why?

chemical messengers

I'M GATEKEEPING BEATER

My car cost 125 dollars

The ceiling is stapled on

The trunk is taped closed

When I brake too hard, paint chips fly off

Someone once told me they drove a beater

It was hard to hear him over the AC

I asked him how much it cost him

Six thousand dollars

This beater's in a different tax bracket

chemical messengers

TRANSPORT ME

Show me a face I haven't seen before

On that rainy sunny day in spring, her voice

transported me

My body was in a classroom

But my spirit was a thousand miles away

A performance

A performance

A performance

On nights like these, I think about the way I

loved you

With my hands

With my teeth

With clamped eyes and closed fists, I loved you

Let me try again

chemical messengers

On nights like these, I think about how you

loved me

With open eyes and wide smiles

You loved me

I sometimes wonder if I ever really loved you

back

I sometimes wonder if I'll ever stop,

What more is there to say?

Our love was like a fission reaction

Intense

Powerful

Over before we knew what happened

Another lie

Another lie

Sometimes I think I still love you

chemical messengers

Sometimes I think I never did

But I still think of you

I think I still miss you

But maybe I just miss the way I felt when I was

with you

A new voice fills the room, bringing me back

My body and spirit are in a classroom My

memories are with you

Maybe a part of them always will be

chemical messengers

LIFE MAKES ITS OWN

METAPHORS

I dropped a mug

It looked intact

But when I picked it up,

it shattered into a million pieces

It's like it hadn't realized it was broken

chemical messengers

THIS WON'T MAKE ME A BETTER ARTIST

We don't know why it works

And it's dangerous

But you'll feel more normal than you ever have

in your life

Don't you want to be normal?

Who wouldn't want to be normal?

chemical messengers

THE FIRST THING WE DID WITH THE FALLEN ANGEL WAS DISSECT IT

We wanted to understand something so

beautiful, so we carefully took it apart

Piece by piece until we knew for sure

That we could never comprehend a body so

celestial

A thousand years ago we would have eaten it

Maybe we'd have learned a different lesson

chemical messengers

DEVON ASKS ME WHY I WRITE POETRY

I tell her it's because I struggle to be understood

So, I just write how I think and call it poetry

What else, what else

Understanding; the quest for, potential memoir

title

That's it, really

I want to be understood

I'm misunderstood because I'm crazy, but I'm

crazy because I'm misunderstood

Snake eats tail

chemical messengers

THIS CAR RUNS ON FAITH

2001 Buick LeSabre custom

I tell the tow driver

I tell the AAA man

I tell the Les Schwab mechanic

I don't remember exactly what the last one told

me but if I had to summarize it in four words:

Your car is fucked.

My dad tells me not to drive the pass because

my transmission's going out

He was saying the same thing eighteen months

ago

chemical messengers

THE ASTEROIDS WILL TAKE US HOME

It's been visible for the last week

Growing ever larger ever closer

Every day, we gather and observe

Every day, we grow closer to realizing that this

will change everything

Every day, we gather and observe

Every day, we realize that, for the moment, this

changes nothing

We graze or we hunt

We fight, we defend

Meanwhile, it grows ever closer

Ever larger

The aftertaste of something much smaller than

me

Imagine dying lucky at the hands of a predator

chemical messengers

Imagine dying with everyone else all at once

Imagine dying

We were animals too

We didn't know what was happening and then it

was happening

In a week, we'll all be dead So, we hunt

Or we graze

We fight and we defend Every day, we gather

And we observe

The asteroid grows ever larger

Ever closer

chemical messengers

WHILE WE'RE ON THE TOPIC OF

ETERNAL DAMNATION

If there's an afterlife, I'll relent on my deathbed

When things start to get bad, I think about my

funeral

I think about the guest list

The eulogy

The epitaph

I LOVE I AM LOVED

On the off chance of eternal damnation, I'll

repent on my deathbed

When things start to get bad, I tell myself I'll

take my lithium

Lately I've been thinking about my funeral

A tragedy

A party in my honor

chemical messengers

And I won't be able to attend

I'm thinking about starting back on my lithium

It doesn't make me feel better about myself but

It does make me feel better

Truthfully, I've never felt better than when there

was heavy metals coursing through my veins

LiHCO3

The chemical abbreviation for my mental

alleviation

I wouldn't have written this if I was taking it

I wouldn't write anything if I was taking it.

I want an open mic funeral

I want all my loved ones to bond over having

known me

chemical messengers

I want the spiderwebs of my actions to make

themselves apparent to those who have been

caught in them

chemical messengers

Exary Valles(left) is a Yakima poet and artist.

they spend their time outside of school reading,

writing, painting, and leaving their mark where

others will see it

chemical messengers

the cover of this book was painted by California

artist Devon Brown

chemical messengers

Printed in the USA
CPSIA information can be obtained
at www.ICGtesting.com
CBHW020504021024
15218CB00023B/558